How to Dazzle at

Writing

Irene Yates

Brilliant
PUBLICATIONS

We hope you and your class enjoy using this book. Other books in the series include:

To find out more details on any of our resources, please log onto our website: www.brilliantpublications.co.uk.

Published by Brilliant Publications,
Unit 10, Sparrow Hall Farm,
Edlesborough, Dunstable, Bedfordshire LU6 2ES

email: info@brilliantpublications.co.uk
website: www.brilliantpublications.co.uk
Tel: 01525 222292

The name Brilliant Publications and its logo are registered trademarks.

Written by Irene Yates
Illustrated by Sarah Hedley

© Irene Yates 1998
Printed ISBN 978 1 897675 45 8
ebook ISBN 978 0 85747 098 0

First published 1998. Reprinted 1999 and 2011.
Printed in the UK
10 9 8 7 6 5 4 3

Contents

Introduction

How to Dazzle at Writing contains 42 photocopiable sheets for use with Key Stage 3 pupils who are working at levels 1-3 of the National Curriculum in English (Scottish levels A-B). The activities are presented in an adolescent-friendly manner and provide a flexible but structured resource for encouraging pupils to write different kinds of material for different reasons, and thus to develop their abilities and extend their basic skills.

It is often the case that pupils of this age feel they are great writing failures because they have difficulty with the mechanics of the task. Many decide that they cannot write because their handwriting or their spelling is poor. The process of writing is actually about two completely different factors – the message and the messenger, the content and the ability to write the message down, the composing and the scripting skills. Quite often, pupils find it very difficult to get beyond the mechanics of 'getting the words down on the paper' to the act of considering the logical order of information or, even, taking care over the formulation of their information. What they need is a build-up of confidence, which comes from the reader, so that they feel they have as much potential as anyone else to make a meaningful communication on paper.

Part of the disaffection of pupils with special needs is the misery of failing time after time. The sheets are designed, with information and questioning, to help those pupils to experience success and achievement. The expectation that the pupil *will* achieve will help to build confidence and competence.

The tasks in this book are kept fairly short, to facilitate concentration. The text on the pages is kept to a minimum, and the content of the pages is applied to contexts that the pupils will find motivating. The extra task at the end of each activity provides reinforcement and enables pupils to use their skills in another way.

How to use the book

The activity pages are designed to supplement any English language activities you pursue in the classroom. They are intended to add to your pupils' knowledge of how the English language works.

They can be used with individual pupils, pairs or very small groups, as the need arises. The text on the pages has been kept as short as possible, so that reluctant or poorer readers will not feel swamped by 'words on the page'. For the same reason, we have used white space and boxes, to help the pupils to understand the sheets easily, and to give them a measure of independence in working through them.

It is not the author's intention that a teacher should expect all the pupils to complete all the sheets, rather that the sheets be used with a flexible approach, so that the book provides a bank of resources that will meet needs as they arise.

Many of the sheets can be modified and extended in very simple ways. The Add-ons can provide a good vehicle for discussion of what has been learned and how it can be applied.

It is essential to keep an open perspective on handwriting and spelling while the pupil is composing. These two factors may be ignored while the pupil is composing and creating, then the pupil should be helped to proofread the first draft, and encouraged to think about the conventions and put them right during the redrafting stage.

The composing process improves enormously with:

- good quality discussion before putting pen to paper

- the promise of 'publication'

- knowledge of an audience that is not 'just' the teacher who is going to mark the work.

Different kinds of writing

There are lots of different kinds of writing. This list is to help me keep track of my ideas. I need never say, 'I can't think of anything to write about!'

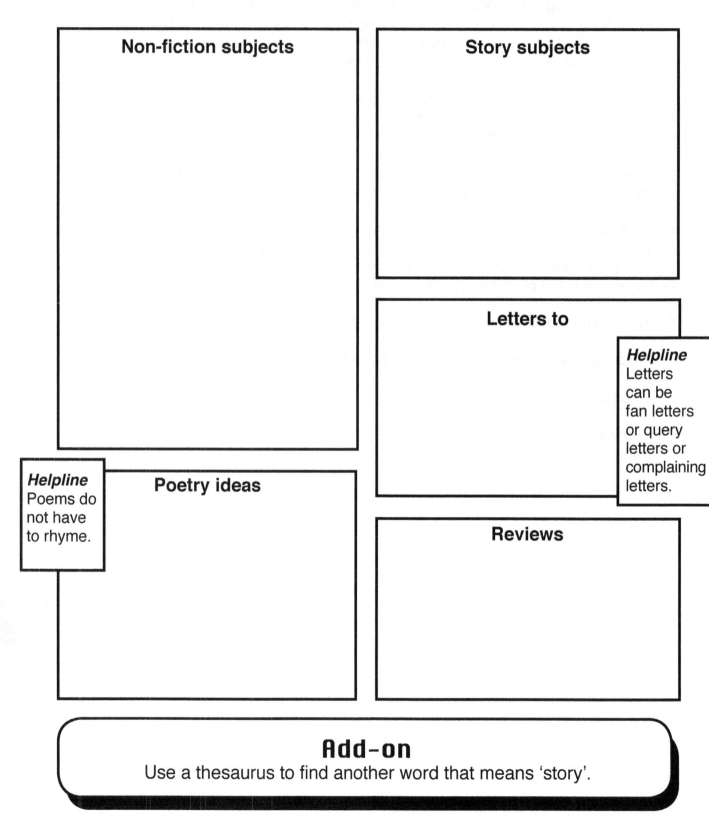

Non-fiction subjects

Story subjects

Letters to

Helpline
Letters can be fan letters or query letters or complaining letters.

Helpline
Poems do not have to rhyme.

Poetry ideas

Reviews

Add-on
Use a thesaurus to find another word that means 'story'.

How to Dazzle at Writing
6

© Irene Yates
This page may be photocopied for use by the purchasing institution only.

Plan a story

My story is about …

It will begin with …

In the middle this will happen …

It will end with …

My main character is:

Description:

Add-on
Look up 'description' in the dictionary.

A good story

What makes a good story? Plan one here.

Give it:

Helpline
Write about something you know about.

A good title:

A good beginning:

A good middle:

A strong ending:

Add-on
How can you make your story even better?

Six questions

There are six questions that you should try to answer when you are writing something.

They are:

Who?   What?   Where?   How?   When?   Why?

Plan some stories by using these questions.

Story 1

Who?	Where?	When?	What?	How?	Why?

Story 2

Who?	Where?	When?	What?	How?	Why?

Add-on
Write one of your stories.

Making notes

You have to practise making notes to be good at it. The rules are easy:

Listen or read with lots of attention.

You don't have to write in 'best' or in proper sentences.

Try to find out the important facts.

You have to be able to read and understand what you have written.

Jot down only the things that matter.

Read an article or a chapter in a reference book or magazine.

Make notes here:

Add-on
Use your notes to write a new piece of non-fiction.

Finding words

There are lots of different words that mean almost the same thing.

Think of four different words for:

said _____ _____ _____ _____

nice _____ _____ _____ _____

big _____ _____ _____ _____

walk _____ _____ _____ _____

eat _____ _____ _____ _____

coat _____ _____ _____ _____

Add-on
Words that mean almost the same are called synonyms.
Have a look at a thesaurus to see lists of synonyms.

Making up a character

Good stories have strong characters. A strong character is someone you will remember after you have finished the story. A strong character is always good enough to write lots of stories about.

Make up your own character.

Fact file
Is your character human/nonhuman?

How old is your character?

Where does your character live?

Description
What does your character look like?

Personality
What is your character like?

Add-on
Think of four different things your character could do.
Which would make the best story?

Telling it how it is

Everywhere you look there is something giving you 'information'.

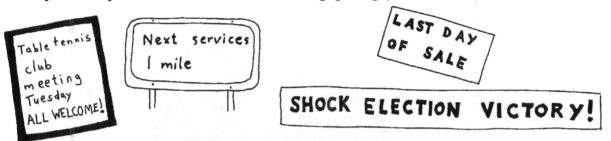

Write your own information reports here:

Newspaper article about a day in history

Notice about a meeting of a sports club	Ad for a new computer game

Add-on
Find five different pieces of information to read.
Rewrite one of them for Teletext.

Mountain bike

Ben's getting a new mountain bike for his birthday.

He wants to know
- how to change gear
- how to look after it
- what he can do on it.

Imagine you're the man in the cycle shop, giving him advice.

This is how to change gear:

This is how to look after it:

This is what it can do:

Add-on
Draw a diagram of a mountain bike and label it.

Cup final

Your granny has won two tickets to the cup final. The good news is she's going to give you one! The bad news is, she's coming with you.

Explain to her what these terms mean.

referee

penalty

off-side

kick-off

half-time

Helpline
Write notes only.

Add-on
Read your explanations to a friend and see if they agree with you.

Pet care

You can have any animal you like as a pet.

What will you choose? _____

Draw a picture of your pet.

Write a list of instructions of how to look after your pet.

Helpline
Where will your pet live? What will you feed it? Where will you get the food?

Add-on
Write instructions for keeping a dog.

Cash to spend

You're a famous pop star. You have all the money in the world. You are going to buy a new home.

Make a list of everything the house you are looking for should have.

Helpline
Think BIG!

Add-on
Make up a title for your best-selling album,
and a name for your group.

Do nothing

Wouldn't it be great to have some time when you had to do absolutely nothing?

Make a list of twenty things that you would not have to do.

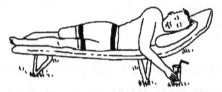

1	11	**Helpline** Think of all the things you hate doing!
2	12	
3	13	
4	14	
5	15	
6	16	
7	17	
8	18	
9	19	
10	20	

Add-on
Can you put your twenty things in order?
Start with the thing you'd least like to do.

Danger!

These boys think it's fun to explore caves, but it's very dangerous.

Write a notice that will keep them out.

Helpline
Think about darkness, falling rocks, the sea, the tide.

Write four things that could happen if they ignore the warning.

1

2

3

4

Add-on
How many sea-shore words can you think of?

Gnash, gnash, gnash

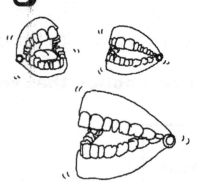

Write down every single thing you can think about on the subject of teeth.

You can make your writing funny or serious, or both. It can be true or made up, or both.

> **Helpline**
> If you know any good teeth or dentist stories, go ahead and put them in!

Add-on
Find out from a reference book what the different types of teeth you have are called. Practise writing the words.

Describe a dinosaur

Nobody else knows, but there's a
dinosaur in the corner of the park.

Describe the dinosaur.

Helpline
Think of a
particular type
of dinosaur.

What happens when your dinosaur disturbs the neighbours?

Add-on
Look up in a reference book the names of as many
dinosaurs as you can find. Practise spelling the words.

What a day!

Pick a day, any day, that stands out in your memory for some reason. Write what happened here.

A day in the life of …

Helpline
It could be a good day or a bad day. Try to write about your feelings.

That day …

Add-on

Try keeping a journal. You don't have to write in it every day –
just on days when big or memorable things happen.

Write a letter

Gary bought a CD that won't play properly.

Write a letter to the shop, complaining.

Gary's address

Shop address

Date

Dear Sir/Madam,

Yours faithfully,

Add-on
What else might you write a letter of complaint about?

Thanks a lot!

Chris has two tickets to a pop concert. The tickets get lost!
On the day of the concert, the police phone to say someone
has handed in the tickets.

Write Chris's letter to the finder, saying thank you.

Chris's address

Finder's address

Date

Dear

Helpline
Write your
letter in
three short
paragraphs.

Many thanks once again.

Best wishes,

Add-on
Do a short review of the pop concert.

Expert

Think about something you are really
'an expert' at doing. It can be anything –
a game, a sport, making tea, collecting
something. Arnold here wants to know all about
your special subject, too.

**Write a letter, telling Arnold everything
you know.**

Dear Arnold,

How to …

Helpline
Try to get your
ideas in order
first.

This is how it goes.

First, you …

Add-on
Draw diagrams and label them, to go with your letter.

Holiday disaster!

Ben has booked a holiday in Moonsville. First there is a delay in the rocket launching. Then the crater he is staying at is dirty and noisy. He is promised air-floating and comet-jumping but they are cancelled.

Write his postcards back to Earth, telling what happened.

Dear Mum,

Dear Tom,

Helpline
Write as much as you can on each postcard.

It doesn't have to be in proper sentences.

Add-on
Write a letter to the Astro-Air Holiday Company, asking for Ben's money back.

School gates

Helpline
Look for details in the picture.

What can you see in the picture?
What is happening? Tell your story out loud to
someone first. Write it here.

Add-on
Write three sentences about going home from your school.

At the match

Helpline
Look for details
in the picture.

What can you see in the picture?
What is happening? Tell your story out loud to
someone first. Write it here.

Add-on
Write a paragraph about a football match you've seen.

Help!

Tell your story out loud to someone first. Then write it here.

Use some of these words:
- danger
- deep
- dive
- fishing
- help
- paddle
- rescue
- river
- water
- young

Add-on
Record your story on to a cassette.

Rescue!

Tell your story out loud to someone first. Then write it here.

Use some of these words:
- ball
- beach
- game
- holiday
- lifeguard
- mouth-to-mouth
- paramedics
- rescue
- helicopter
- unconscious

Add-on
Record your story on to a cassette/CD or computer.

Choose a character

Choose a character you know from a TV programme, a film, a comic or a book.

Put the character in a situation with you (at your home or school, or somewhere you go).

Write the story here.

Add-on
Write or record what it is about your character
that you really like.

Imagine you're a goldfish ...

Think about your favourite place. Now, imagine you're a goldfish in a bowl, and describe the place as the goldfish senses it.

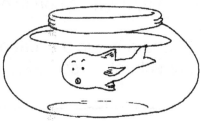

My favourite place is:

This is what it looks like from the goldfish bowl:

This is what it sounds like:

This is what it smells like:

Add-on
What if you were a dog instead of a goldfish?
Write what you see, hear, smell and feel.

Where in the world?

This is your ticket to anywhere in the world. Where will you go?

Ticket to _____

Name of
passenger _____

Will you fly? Will you go by sea? By land?

Will you go alone or take a friend?

Collect your ticket and *take off!*

Helpline
You can write about somewhere you have been, or somewhere you have heard or read about.

Write what happens here.

Add-on
Find the place you choose on a map of the world.

I'd like to be ...

If you could be anyone in the world, who would you like to be?

Someone real?

Someone made up?

Someone you know?

Someone you'll never meet?

I would be …

How would your life be different?
What would happen?

Write your story here.

Add-on
Write a paragraph about what it's like to be you.

What if ...?

What if you are suddenly beamed-up to another planet? What things would you miss about your life on Earth?

Write what things you would miss here.

Helpline
Think about *all* the things that are good about your life. Try to say *why* you would miss them.

Add-on
Write about three things you would definitely *not* miss.

Moonbase

Scientists have discovered water on the
moon. This means there may be life there.
What kind of life do you think it could be?

Give your moon-life a name:

**Draw your moon-life
here:**

Describe it:

**What will happen when the *Moon Explorer Rocket* lands and
Astro-Commander Jones meets your moon-life?**

Add-on
Practise spelling these words:
astronaut, galaxy, comet, star, spaceship.

Ghostly encounter

This is a haunted house. Your friend has bet you that you won't stay in the house all night. But you reckon you will.

What happens?

Write your story here.

Add-on
Tell a ghost story that you have read or seen on film.

Jo's bike

What Jo wants more than anything
in the world is a mountain bike.
Everybody else has one. But Dad
says he can't afford one. Jo tries not
to sulk but then, one day, …

Write your story here.

Helpline
Did something
happen to
change Jo's
luck?

Add-on
Practise spelling these words:
bike, tyre, wheel, saddle, handlebars, brakes.

Help, I've shrunk!

Imagine one day you go to school and, just as you go in, you shrink. Suddenly you're less than half your real size.

What do you do?

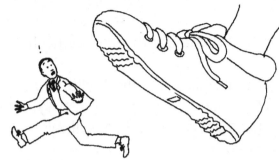

Write what happens here.

Helpline
How are you going to fit at your desk?

Add-on
What if the opposite happened,
and you grew to twice your real size?

Haiku

A haiku is a Japanese poem. It only has three lines. You write it in syllables.

The first line has five syllables.
The second line has seven syllables.
The third line has five syllables.

Here are two examples:

> **Street corner**
> Everybody meets.
> We gossip and have a laugh,
> Just hanging around.

> **Sunday**
> Can't find anything
> to do, except walk by the
> river, and chase dreams.

Write you own haiku poems:

Video

_____

_____

Sport

_____

_____

I like

_____

_____

I hate

_____

_____

Add-on

Read your haiku poems out loud to someone else.
Record the group's best haiku poems.

Acrostics

How to write an acrostic poem:
- choose a topic
- write the word downwards
- write a phrase or sentence against each letter.

Here are some examples:

B eetles are as
U gly as sin, but
G reat to draw.

G houls and ghosts
H aunt
O ld places,
S triking
T error in your heart!

Write your own acrostic poems here.

Helpline
Here are some topics you could try:
- spider
- bikes
- exercise
- fun day.

Add-on
Choose your best acrostic poem and copy it out in best writing.
Illustrate it for display.

Cinquains

A cinquain is a poem which has only five lines and eleven words. The rules are:

Line one   –   one word
Line two   –   two words
Line three   –   three words
Line four   –   four words
Line five   –   one word

Here are some examples:

Goal
The
Crowd roars
As I slice
The ball into the
Net.

Video
I
Watch horror
Movies all night,
Too scared to fall
Asleep!

Write your own cinquains here:

Add-on
Make a display of your group's poems.
Read them out loud.

Pop song

You are a famous pop star and you write all your own songs.

Choose a tune that you know well, and write new words to fit it.

Helpline
Make your song about something different.

Add-on
Record your song on to a cassette tape/CD or computer.

Conflict!

Two boys are having an argument.
- Who are they?
- What are they saying to each other?

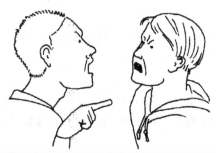

Write a scene for a play.

Scene (when and where):

Boy 1: (quietly)

Boy 2: (   )

Boy 1: (   )

Boy 2: (   )

Boy 1: (   )

Boy 2: (   )

Boy 1: (   )

Add-on
If you haven't finished the scene, turn over the page
and carry on writing.

TV best

Write a review of your favourite TV programme.

My favourite TV programme is:

What kind of programme is it?

Who appears in it?

What happens in it?

Tell your favourite episode here:

Add-on
Make up a page like this one about the programme
you hate most in the whole world.

Video review

Think of a video you really like and write a review of it.

Title:

Main characters:

I like this video because …

My favourite scene is:

Add-on
Read your review to someone who has seen the same video.
Do they agree with you?

Film review

Think of a film you really like and write a review of it.

Title:

Main characters:	Played by:

Where the story is set:

What the story is about:

I like this film because …

Add-on
Which do you think is the best scene in the film? Why?

Comic story

Choose a picture strip story that you
like from a comic or magazine.

Retell the story here.

This is why I like this story:

Add-on
Make one of your own stories into a picture strip.

Lightning Source UK Ltd.
Milton Keynes UK
UKOW07f1043141217
314460UK00002B/40/P